February 2012

DOD SUPPLY CHAIN

Suspect Counterfeit Electronic Parts Can Be Found on Internet Purchasing Platforms

G A O

Accountability ★ Integrity ★ Reliability

GAO-12-375

GAO
Accountability * Integrity * Reliability

Highlights

Highlights of GAO-12-375, a report to the Committee on Armed Services, U.S. Senate

DOD SUPPLY CHAIN

Suspect Counterfeit Electronic Parts Can Be Found on Internet Purchasing Platforms

Why GAO Did This Study

Counterfeit parts—generally the misrepresentation of parts' identity or pedigree—can seriously disrupt the Department of Defense (DOD) supply chain, harm weapon systems integrity, and endanger troops' lives. In a November testimony (GAO-12-213T), GAO summarized preliminary observations from its investigation into the purchase and authenticity testing of selected, military-grade electronic parts that may enter the DOD supply chain. As requested, this report presents GAO's final findings on this issue. The results are based on a nongeneralizable sample and cannot be used to make inferences about the extent to which parts are being counterfeited.

GAO created a fictitious company and gained membership to two Internet platforms providing access to vendors selling military-grade electronic parts. GAO requested quotes from numerous vendors to purchase a total of 16 parts from three categories: (1) authentic part numbers for obsolete and rare parts; (2) authentic part numbers with postproduction date codes (date codes after the last date the part was manufactured); and (3) bogus, or fictitious, part numbers that are not associated with any authentic parts. To determine whether the parts received were counterfeit, GAO contracted with a qualified, independent testing lab for full component authentication analysis of the first two categories of parts, but not the third (bogus) category. Part numbers have been altered for reporting purposes.

GAO is not making recommendations in this report.

View GAO-12-375. For more information, contact Richard J. Hillman at (202) 512-6722 or hillmanr@gao.gov or Timothy Persons at (202) 512-6522 or personst@gao.gov.

What GAO Found

Suspect counterfeit and bogus—part numbers that are not associated with any authentic parts—military-grade electronic parts can be found on Internet purchasing platforms, as none of the 16 parts vendors provided to GAO were legitimate. "Suspect counterfeit," which applies to the first two categories of parts that were tested, is the strongest term used by an independent testing lab, signifying a potential violation of intellectual property rights, copyrights, or trademark laws, or misrepresentation to defraud or deceive. After submitting requests for quotes on both platforms, GAO received responses from 396 vendors, of which 334 were located in China; 25 in the United States; and 37 in other countries, including the United Kingdom and Japan. Of the 16 parts purchased, vendors usually responded within a day. GAO selected the first of any vendor among those offering the lowest prices that provided enough information to purchase a given part, generally within 2 weeks. Under GAO's selection methodology, all 16 parts were provided by vendors in China.

All Parts GAO Received Were Suspect Counterfeit or Bogus

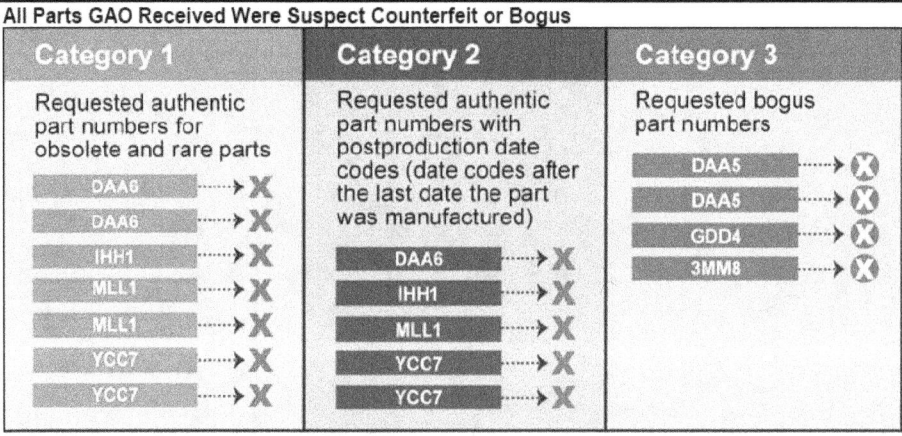

Category 1	Category 2	Category 3
Requested authentic part numbers for obsolete and rare parts	Requested authentic part numbers with postproduction date codes (date codes after the last date the part was manufactured)	Requested bogus part numbers
DAA6 ----→ X		DAA5 ----→ ⊗
DAA6 ----→ X		DAA5 ----→ ⊗
IHH1 ----→ X		GDD4 ----→ ⊗
MLL1 ----→ X	DAA6 ----→ X	3MM8 ----→ ⊗
MLL1 ----→ X	IHH1 ----→ X	
YCC7 ----→ X	MLL1 ----→ X	
YCC7 ----→ X	YCC7 ----→ X	
	YCC7 ----→ X	

X - Suspect counterfeit part   ⊗ - Bogus part

Source: GAO analysis of independent laboratory test results.

Note: Part numbers shown have been altered from the part numbers used for purchasing.

Specifically, all 12 of the parts received after GAO requested rare part numbers or postproduction date codes were suspect counterfeit, according to the testing lab. Multiple authentication tests, ranging from inspection with electron microscopes to X-ray analysis, revealed that the parts had been re-marked to display the part numbers and manufacturer logos of authentic parts. Other features were found to be deficient from military standards, such as the metallic composition of certain pieces. For the parts requested using postproduction date codes, the vendors also altered date markings to represent the parts as newer than when they were last manufactured, as verified by the parts' makers. Finally, after submitting requests for bogus parts using invalid part numbers, GAO purchased four parts from four vendors, which shows their willingness to supply parts that do not technically exist.

Contents

Abbreviations

DLA	Defense Logistics Agency
DOD	Department of Defense
RTS	resistance to solvents
SEM	scanning electron microscopy
XRF	X-ray florescence

United States Government Accountability Office
Washington, DC 20548

February 21, 2012

The Honorable Carl Levin
Chairman
The Honorable John McCain
Ranking Member
Committee on Armed Services
United States Senate

Counterfeit parts—generally the misrepresentation of parts' identity or pedigree—have the potential to seriously disrupt the Department of Defense (DOD) supply chain, delay missions, affect the integrity of weapon systems, and ultimately endanger the lives of our troops. Almost anything is at risk of being counterfeited, from fasteners used on aircraft to electronics used on missile guidance systems. There can be many sources of counterfeit parts as DOD draws from a large network of global suppliers.[1]

In 2011, we reported that the increase in counterfeit electronic parts is one of several potential barriers DOD faces in addressing parts quality problems.[2] More recently, you asked about the availability of counterfeit parts on Internet platforms commonly used to buy hard-to-find military-grade electronic parts, including those used in weapon systems. In a November testimony, we summarized preliminary observations from our investigation into the purchase and authenticity testing of selected, military-grade electronic parts that may enter the DOD supply chain.[3] This report presents our final findings on this issue.

In conducting this investigation, we created a fictitious company to gain access to Internet platforms that provide access to vendors selling

---

[1] GAO, *Defense Supplier Base: DOD Should Leverage Ongoing Initiatives in Developing Its Program to Mitigate Risk of Counterfeit Parts*, GAO-10-389 (Washington, D.C.: Mar. 29, 2010).

[2] GAO, *Space and Missile Defense Acquisitions: Periodic Assessment Needed to Correct Parts Quality Problems in Major Programs*, GAO-11-404 (Washington, D.C.: June 24, 2011).

[3] GAO, *DOD Supply Chain: Preliminary Observations Indicate That Counterfeit Electronic Parts Can Be Found on Internet Purchasing Platforms*, GAO-12-213T (Washington, D.C.: Nov. 8, 2011).

GAO-12-375 Suspect Counterfeit Parts

military-grade electronic parts. Our company included a fictitious owner and employees, mailing and e-mail addresses, a website, and a listing on the Central Contractor Registration.[4] We attempted to purchase memberships to three Internet platforms that were of interest to this committee. One platform granted us membership despite not receiving all requested supporting documentation, the second granted us membership after we supplied the requested documentation as well as fictitious business references, and the third denied our request for membership even after we provided all documentation and references. None of the platforms contacted our references. We then requested quotes from vendors on both platforms to purchase a total of 16 parts from three categories: (1) authentic part numbers for obsolete and rare parts; (2) authentic part numbers with postproduction date codes (date codes after the last date the part was manufactured); and (3) bogus, or fictitious, part numbers that are not associated with any authentic parts. Using a list of four authentic part numbers this committee provided, we purchased 7 parts from the first category and 5 parts from the second (for which we altered only the date code). We independently verified with the Defense Logistics Agency (DLA) that these part numbers were used for military applications using DLA's Federal Logistics Information System and by interviewing DLA officials.[5] We used three invalid part numbers provided by the committee, which altered portions of existing part numbers that identify certain performance specifications, to purchase the 4 bogus parts. We then confirmed with DLA and selected part manufacturers that the numbers we developed were invalid. We altered all part numbers for reporting purposes.

We requested parts from vendors that were new in original packaging, not refurbished, and had no mixed date codes. We selected the first vendor among those offering the lowest prices that provided enough information, such as name, addresses, and payment method, to make a purchase. We attempted to avoid using the same vendor more than once unless no other vendor responded to our request; however, vendors may operate under more than one name. We did not attempt to verify the

---

[4] The Central Contractor Registration is the primary contractor registrant database for the U.S. federal government. The Central Contractor Registration collects, validates, stores, and disseminates data in support of agency acquisition missions.

[5] DLA's Federal Logistics Information System via the World Wide Web provides general information about more than 8 million supply items used by the U.S. government and North Atlantic Treaty Organization (NATO) allies.

GAO-12-375 Suspect Counterfeit Parts

independence of any vendor before we made our purchases. Finally, we contracted with the SMT Corp. for full component authentication analysis.[6] For details on this analysis, see appendix I.

The results of this investigation are based on the use of a nongeneralizable sample, and these results cannot be used to make inferences about the extent to which parts are being counterfeited. We conducted this investigation from August 2011 to February 2012 in accordance with standards prescribed by the Council of the Inspectors General on Integrity and Efficiency.

Suspect Counterfeit Electronic Parts Can Be Found on Internet Purchasing Platforms

As shown in figure 1, each of the 16 parts we purchased was either suspect counterfeit or bogus. Specifically, all 12 of the parts we received after requesting authentic part numbers (either with valid or invalid date codes) were suspect counterfeit, according to SMT Corp. In addition, vendors provided us with 4 bogus parts after we requested invalid part numbers, which demonstrates their willingness to sell parts that do not technically exist. The following sections detail our findings for each of the three categories of parts we purchased.

Under our selection methodology, the 16 parts we purchased were provided by 13 vendors in China. After submitting requests for quotes on both platforms, we received responses from 396 vendors, of which 334 were located in China; 25 in the United States; and 37 in other countries, including the United Kingdom and Japan. All 40 of the responses we received for the bogus part numbers were from vendors located in China (6 of these vendors also offered to sell us parts for the authentic part numbers we requested). We selected the first of any vendor among those offering the lowest prices that provided enough information to purchase a given part, generally within 2 weeks.[7] As such, 3 vendors each supplied 2 parts and 10 vendors each supplied 1 part. We sent 13 payments to Shenzhen, 2 payments to Shantou, and 1 payment to Beijing. Despite operating under different company names, 2 vendors provided us with

---

[6] We selected SMT Corp. as the independent, full component authentication testing laboratory based on its (1) ability to conduct 100 percent component inspection with transmission X-rays, (2) use of a patented heated solvent test, and (3) use of scanning electron microscopy to detect surface abnormalities as well as doing spectroscopic analysis of surface material on the components.

[7] These vendors usually responded to our initial requests for quotes within a day.

identical information for sending payment (name of representative and contact information). There could be a number of explanations for this, ranging from legitimate (the vendors handle payments through the same banker or accountant) to potentially deceptive (same individuals representing themselves as multiple companies). Thirteen parts were then shipped from Shenzhen and 3 from Hong Kong.

Figure 1: Status of Parts Purchased and Tested

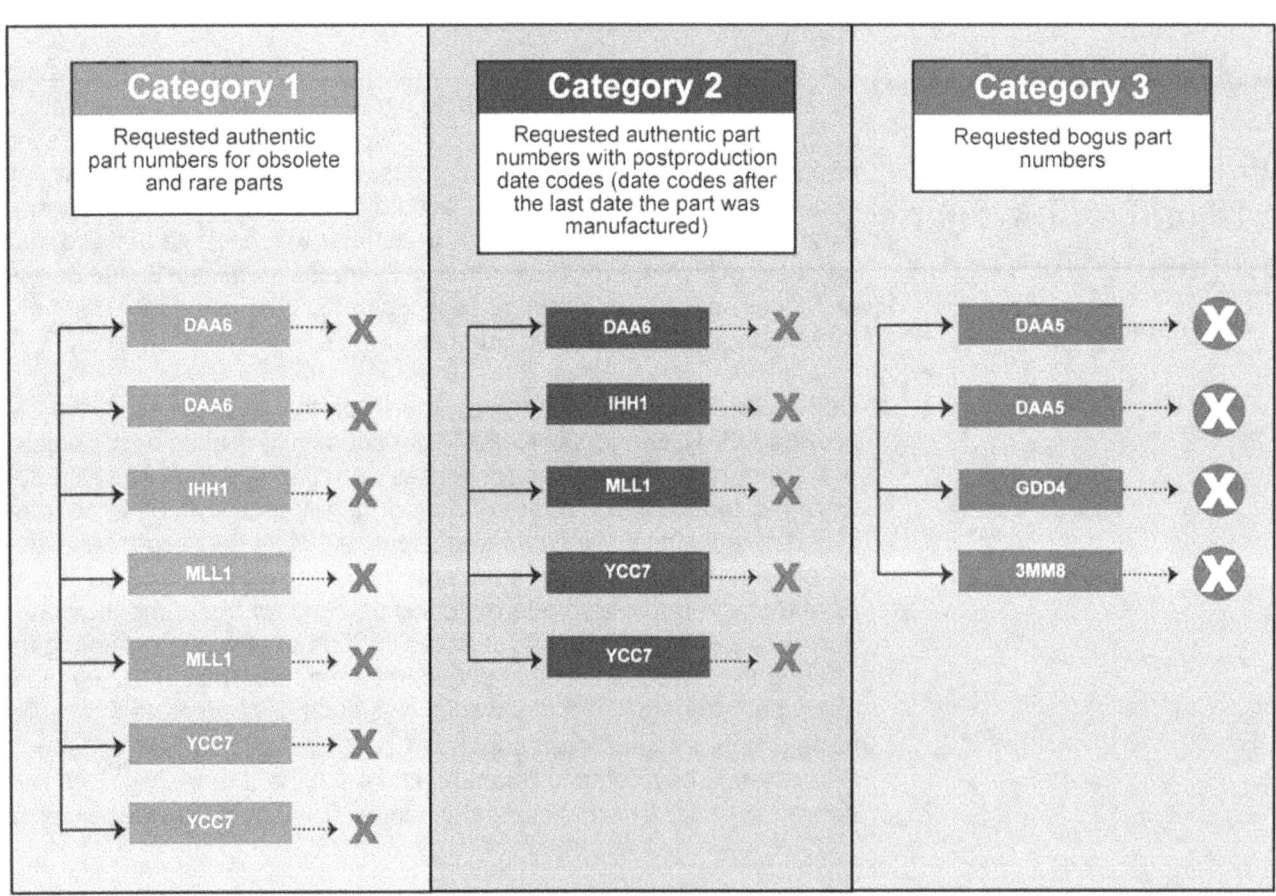

X   - Suspect counterfeit part

Ⓧ   - Bogus part

Source: GAO analysis of SMT test results.

Note: Part numbers shown have been altered from the part numbers used for purchasing.

Category 1: Authentic Part Numbers for Obsolete or Rare Parts

All seven of the obsolete or rare parts that SMT Corp. tested were suspected counterfeits. Each part failed multiple component authentication analyses, including visual, chemical, X-ray, and microscopic testing. The parts were purchased from five different vendors. Figure 2 provides photos and detailed test results for each part.

Category 1 Requested authentic part numbers for obsolete and rare parts							
Analysis performed	**DAA6**	**DAA6**	**IHH1**	**MLL1**	**MLL1**	**YCC7**	**YCC7**
Visual Inspection	Fail ☒	Fail ☒	Fail ☒	Fail ☒	Fail ☒	Fail ☒	Fail ☒
Resistance to Solvents (RTS) and Scrape Test	N/A	N/A	Fail ☒	N/A	N/A	Pass ☑	Pass ☑
Package Configuration and Dimensions	Pass ☑	Pass ☑	Pass ☑	Pass ☑	Pass ☑	Pass ☑	Fail ☒
X-Ray Florescence Elemental Analysis	Fail ☒	Fail ☒	Pass ☑	Fail ☒	Fail ☒	Pass ☑	Pass ☑
Real-Time X-ray Analysis	Pass ☑	Fail ☒	Pass ☑	Pass ☑	Pass ☑	Fail ☒	Pass ☑
Scanning Electron Microscopy (SEM) Analysis	Fail ☒	Fail ☒	Fail ☒	Pass ☑	Pass ☑	Fail ☒	Fail ☒
Solderability Test	Pass ☑	Pass ☑	Pass ☑	Pass ☑	Pass ☑	Pass ☑	Pass ☑
Dynasolve Test	N/A	N/A	Fail ☒	N/A	N/A	N/A	Fail ☒
Delidding and Die Microscopy	Fail ☒	Fail ☒	Fail ☒	Fail ☒	Fail ☒	Fail ☒	Pass ☑
Suspect counterfeit	**Yes**	**Yes**	**Yes**	**Yes**	**Yes**	**Yes**	**Yes**

Source: GAO analysis of SMT test results.

Note: Part numbers shown have been altered from the part numbers used for purchasing. N/A indicates that the analysis was not performed because the unique properties of the part render the test inapplicable or prevent the test from being performed.

DAA6 (two parts purchased). Both purchases made using part number DAA6 contained samples that failed multiple authentication analyses, leading SMT Corp. to conclude that the parts were suspect counterfeit.

Both parts were purchased from different vendors using the same part number, but were not identical, as shown in figure 2. An authentic part with this part number is an operational amplifier that may be commonly found in the Army and Air Force's Joint Surveillance and Target Attack Radar System; the Air Force's F-15 Eagle fighter plane; and the Air Force, Navy, and Marine Corps's Maverick AGM-65A missile. If authentic, this part converts input voltages into output voltages that can be hundreds to thousands of times larger. Failure can lead to unreliable operation of several components (e.g., integrated circuits) in the system and poses risks to the function of the system where the parts reside.

The part we received from one vendor failed four of seven authentication analyses. Visual inspection found inconsistencies, including different or missing markings and scratches, which suggested that samples were re-marked. Scanning electron microscopy (SEM) analysis revealed further evidence of re-marking. X-ray fluorescence (XRF) testing of the samples revealed that the leads contain no lead (Pb) instead of the 3 percent lead (Pb) required by military specifications.[8,9] Five samples were chosen for delidding, which exposes parts' die, because of their side marking inconsistencies. While all five samples had the same die, the die markings were inconsistent.[10] According to SMT Corp., die markings in components manufactured within the same date and lot code should be consistent. Finally, the devices found in the first lot tested went into "last time buy" status in 2001, meaning that the parts were misrepresented as newer than they actually were. The manufacturer confirmed this status and added that the part marking did not match its marking scheme, meaning that the date code marked on the samples would not be possible.

---

[8] XRF analyzers quickly and nondestructively determine the elemental composition of materials commonly found in microelectronic devices. Each of the elements present in a sample produces a unique set of characteristic x-rays that reveals the chemistry of the sample in a manner analogous to a fingerprint. A lead is an electrical connection consisting of a length of wire or soldering pad that comes from a device. Leads are used for physical support, to transfer power, to probe circuits, and to transmit information.

[9] DOD, *DOD Performance Specification for Integrated Circuits (Microcircuits) Manufacturing*, MIL-PRF-38535J (Dec. 28, 2010).

[10] A die is a small wafer of semiconducting material on which a functional circuit is fabricated.

The part received from the second vendor failed five of seven authentication analyses. Visual inspection again found inconsistencies, including additional markings on about half the samples. Further, scratches and reconditioned leads indicated that the parts were removed from a working environment—that is, not new as we requested. SEM analysis corroborated these findings. As with the other DAA6 part, XRF testing revealed that the leads contain no lead (Pb). X-rays revealed different sized die, and delidding revealed that the die were differently marked.

IHH1 (one part purchased). The purchase made using part number IHH1 contained samples that failed five of nine authentication analyses, leading SMT Corp. to conclude that the part was suspect counterfeit. An authentic part with this part number is a multiplexer, which allows electronic signals from several different sources to be checked at one location. It has been used in at least 63 different DOD weapon systems, including the Air Force Special Operations Forces' AC-130H Gunship aircraft, the Air Force's B-2B aircraft, and the Navy's E-2C Hawkeye aircraft. If at least one of the specific signals is critical to the successful operation of the system, then failure could pose a risk to the system overall.

Visual inspection revealed numerous issues, including color differences in the top and bottom of the part's surfaces, suggesting resurfacing and re-marking. Large amounts of scuffs and scratches, foreign debris, and substandard leads were also found. The part also failed resistance to solvents (RTS) testing when it resulted in removal of resurfacing material. Further, Dynasolve testing (additional RTS testing) revealed remnants of a completely different manufacturer and part number. SEM showed evidence of lapping, which is the precise removal of a part's material to produce the desired dimensions, finish, or shape. Finally, delidding showed die that were similar but insufficiently marked to determine whether they matched the authentic part number. However, because of the failure of the Dynasolve testing, the die cannot be correct.

MLL1 (two parts purchased). Both purchases made using part number MLL1 contained a number of samples that failed three of seven authentication analyses, leading SMT Corp. to conclude that the parts were suspect counterfeit. Both parts were purchased from different vendors using the same part number, but were not identical, as shown in figure 2. An authentic part with this number is a voltage regulator that may be commonly found in military systems such as the Air Force's KC-130 Hercules aircraft, the Navy's F/A-18E Super Hornet fighter plane, the

Marine Corps's V-22 Osprey aircraft, and the Navy's SSN-688 Los Angeles Class nuclear-powered attack submarine. If authentic, these parts provide accurate power voltage to segments of the system they serve. Failure can lead to unreliable operation of several components (e.g., integrated circuits) in the system and poses risks to the function of the system where the parts reside.

The parts received from both vendors failed the same authentication analyses. Visual inspection was performed on all evidence samples from both purchases. Different color epoxy seals were noted within both lots, according to SMT Corp., which is common in suspect counterfeit devices because many date and lot codes are re-marked to create a uniform appearance. Moreover, XRF testing of the samples revealed that the leads contain no lead (Pb); according to military performance standards, leads should be alloyed with at least 3 percent of lead (Pb).[11] Further, XRF data between the top and bottom of the lead revealed inconsistencies in chemical composition, leading SMT Corp. to conclude that the leads were extended with the intention to deceive. Microscopic inspection revealed that different revision numbers of the die and differences in various die markings were found even though the samples were advertised to be from the same lot and date code. Commonly, components manufactured within the same date and lot code will have the same die revisions. According to SMT Corp.'s report, the manufacturer also stated that "it is very unusual to have two die runs in a common assembly lot. This is suspicious." Finally, the devices found in the first lot tested went into "last time buy" status—an end-of-life designation—on September 4, 2001, meaning that the parts were misrepresented as newer than they actually were. The manufacturer confirmed this status and added that the part marking did not match its marking scheme, meaning that the date code marked on the samples would not be possible.

YCC7 (two parts purchased). Both purchases made using part number YCC7 contained samples that failed several authentication analyses, leading SMT Corp. to conclude that the parts were suspect counterfeit. Both parts were purchased from different vendors using the same part number. An authentic part with this part number is a memory chip that

---

[11] DOD, *DOD Performance Specification for Integrated Circuits (Microcircuits) Manufacturing.*

has been used in at least 41 different DOD weapons systems, including the ballistic missile early warning system, the Air Force's Peacekeeper missile and B-1B aircraft, the Navy's Trident submarine and Arleigh Burke class of guided missile destroyer, and the Marine Corps's Harrier aircraft. Failure of the chip, if not redundant, could pose risk to the overall system.

The part we received from one vendor failed four of seven authentication analyses. Visual inspection identified numerous issues, including bent or misshapen leads and lead ends and deformed, less-detailed logos of the claimed manufacturer. X-ray analysis revealed that various parts in the samples contained different sized die. SEM analysis showed that surface material had been precisely removed to allow for re-marking. Finally, delidding of two samples revealed die that were marked from a competitor manufacturer with a different part number than the one we requested. In addition, one die was marked with a 1986 copyright, while the other was labeled 1992.

The part received from the second vendor failed four of nine authentication analyses. Visual inspection showed evidence of re-marking, with the color of the top surfaces of samples not matching the color of the bottom surfaces. Some samples displayed faded markings while others were blank and had heavy scuff marks to suggest resurfacing. The markings were also not as clear and consistently placed as manufacturer-etched markings would be. Leads were substandard in quality, had been refurbished, and were not as thick as specified. Further, SEM showed evidence of lapping. Finally, the samples responded inconsistently to Dynasolve testing.

Category 2: Authentic Part Numbers with Postproduction Date Codes

Similarly, all five of the parts we received and tested after requesting legitimate part numbers but specifying postproduction date codes were also suspected counterfeit, according to SMT Corp. By fulfilling our requests, the four vendors that provided these parts represented them as several years newer than the date the parts were last manufactured, as verified by the part manufacturers. Figure 3 provides photos and detailed test results.

Category 2 Requested authentic part numbers with postproduction date codes (date codes after the last date the part was manufactured)					
Analysis performed	**DAA6**	**IHH1**	**MLL1**	**YCC7**	**YCC7**
Visual Inspection	Fail [X]	Fail [X]	Fail [X]	Fail [X]	Fail [X]
Resistance to Solvents (RTS) and Scrape Test	N/A	Fail [X]	N/A	Fail [X]	Fail [X]
Package Configuration and Dimensions	Pass [✓]	Pass [✓]	Pass [✓]	Pass [✓]	Pass [✓]
X-Ray Florescence Elemental Analysis	Fail [X]	Pass [✓]	Fail [X]	Pass [✓]	Pass [✓]
Real-Time X-ray Analysis	Pass [✓]	Fail [X]	Pass [✓]	Pass [✓]	Pass [✓]
Scanning Electron Microscopy (SEM) Analysis	Fail [X]	Fail [X]	Fail [X]	Fail [X]	Fail [X]
Solderability Test	Pass [✓]	Fail [X]	Pass [✓]	Pass [✓]	Pass [✓]
Dynasolve Test	N/A	Fail [X]	N/A	N/A	Pass [✓]
Delidding and Die Microscopy	Fail [X]	Fail [X]	Fail [X]	Pass [✓]	Pass [✓]
Suspect counterfeit	**Yes**	**Yes**	**Yes**	**Yes**	**Yes**

Source: GAO analysis of SMT tst results.

Note: Part numbers shown have been altered from the part numbers used for purchasing. N/A indicates that the analysis was not performed because the unique properties of the part render the test inapplicable or prevent the test from being performed.

DAA6 (one part purchased). The purchase made using part number DAA6 contained samples that failed four of seven authentication analyses, leading SMT Corp. to conclude that the part was suspect counterfeit. Surfaces on the parts in the evidence lots were found to have scratches similar to suspect counterfeit devices that have been re-marked, as confirmed by both visual inspection and SEM analysis. In addition, the quality of exterior markings, including a lack of consistency between the manufacturer's logo, was lower than would be expected for authentic devices. Tooling marks were also found on the bottom of all components within the evidence lot; these marks suggest that the components were pulled from a working environment. Further inspection led SMT Corp. to conclude that many samples with refurbished leads were extended with the intention to deceive. Moreover, XRF analysis revealed the leads contain no lead (Pb) instead of the 3 percent lead (Pb) required by military specifications.[12] Delidding revealed that the die, while correct for this device, were inconsistent. As previously stated, multiple die runs are considered suspicious. Finally, some of the samples went into "last time buy" status in 2001, despite the fact that we requested parts from 2005 or later and the vendor agreed to provide parts from 2010 or later.

IHH1 (one part purchased). The purchase made using part number IHH1 contained samples that failed seven of nine authentication analyses, leading SMT Corp. to conclude that the part was suspect counterfeit. The part we received was supplied by a different vendor than the one that supplied the IHH1 part shown in figure 2. Visual inspection revealed numerous issues, including mismatching surface colors, many scratches and scuffs, foreign debris, and leads that were not uniformly aligned. SEM also showed evidence of lapping. RTS testing resulted in removal of resurfacing material, and surfaces faded when exposed to Dynasolve, which should not occur. Further, samples did not solder properly. Finally, X-rays indicated that different die were used within the samples. This was confirmed in delidding, which revealed inconsistencies in size, shape, and date markings. Of the two types of die found in the sample, one does not match the authentic part number.

MLL1 (one part purchased). The purchase made using part number MLL1 contained samples that failed four of seven authentication analyses, leading SMT Corp. to conclude that the part was suspect

---

[12] DOD, *DOD Performance Specification for Integrated Circuits (Microcircuits) Manufacturing.*

counterfeit. The part we received was supplied by a different vendor than the ones who supplied the MLL1 parts shown in figure 2. Visual inspection revealed scuffs and scratches indicative of re-marking, which was also seen in SEM analysis. Different colored epoxy seals and variegated sizes and colors of the center mounting slug were also seen. Leads also showed evidence of being refurbished with the intent to deceive. XRF testing of the samples revealed that the leads contain no lead (Pb); according to military performance standards, leads should be alloyed with at least 3 percent of lead (Pb).[13] Delidding revealed that die, though similar, had markings indicating different revisions, which is uncommon for die manufactured in the same date code. Finally, the devices went into "last time buy" status in 2001, whereas the tested parts showed a date code indicating they were made in 2008. The manufacturer confirmed this status.

YCC7 (two parts purchased). The two purchases made from different vendors using part number YCC7 contained samples that failed several authentication analyses, leading SMT Corp. to conclude that they were suspect counterfeit. The part we received from one vendor failed three of eight authentication analyses. Visual inspection identified numerous issues, including different colored surfaces that suggest re-marking and unknown residues that indicate improper handling or storage. SEM analysis showed that surface material had been precisely removed to allow for re-marking, similarly to a YCC7 part with legitimate date codes tested above. Further, according to the manufacturer, the legitimate version of this part was last shipped in 2003, whereas the tested part showed a manufacturing date code of 2006. RTS testing resulted in removal of the part marking.

The part received from the second vendor failed three of nine authentication analyses. Visual inspection detected numerous issues, including different colored surfaces that suggest re-marking. The markings were also substandard, lacking clarity and consistency in placement. RTS testing removed part markings, further suggesting re-marking. SEM showed evidence of lapping. Delidding revealed die that were consistent with the authentic part, but the date code showed evidence of re-marking to make them appear as if they had come from a

---

[13] DOD, *DOD Performance Specification for Integrated Circuits (Microcircuits) Manufacturing.*

homogenous lot. Finally, the manufacturer verified that it last shipped this part in 2003, whereas our samples were marked 2007, which according to SMT Corp., could not be possible.

Category 3: Bogus Part Numbers

We received offers from 40 vendors in China to supply parts using invalid part numbers, and we purchased four parts from four vendors to determine whether they would in fact supply bogus parts. (See fig. 4.) These were different vendors than the ones that supplied us with the suspect counterfeit parts. The invalid numbers were based on actual part numbers, but certain portions that define a part's performance specifications were changed. For example, one of our invalid numbers was for an actual voltage regulator but that operated at bogus specifications. None of the invalid part numbers were listed in DLA's Federal Logistics Information System and, according to selected manufacturers, none are associated with parts that have ever been manufactured. As such, we did not send the parts to SMT Corp. for authentication analysis.

Figure 4: Photos of Parts Received Despite Request for Invalid Part Numbers

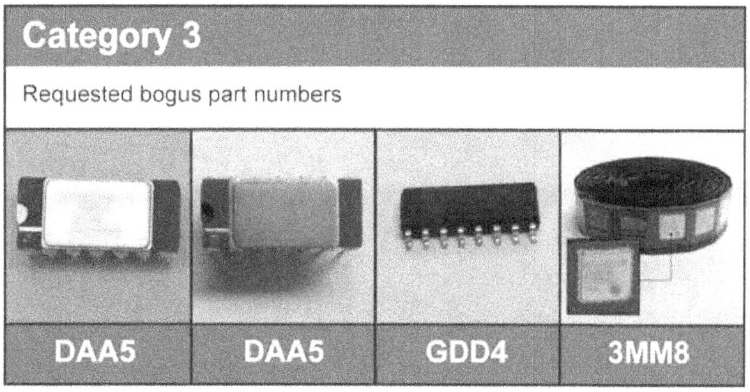

Source: GAO

Note: Part numbers shown have been altered from the part numbers used for purchasing.

We received the four bogus parts after requesting invalid part numbers DAA5, GDD4, and 3MM8. We made two orders using DAA5, one from each Internet purchasing platform, which were fulfilled by different vendors. The parts we received from each vendor appeared similar, as shown in figure 4. The similarity may be due to a number of factors. For example, the vendors could have simply ignored the invalid portion of the part numbers we requested (they did not contact us to inform us that the numbers were invalid). Another possible explanation could be that the parts happened to be fulfilled by the same vendor operating under two different names.

In furtherance of our investigation to determine the willingness of firms to provide us bogus parts, we created a totally fictitious part number that was not based on an actual part number and requested quotations over one Internet platform. We received an offer to supply the part from one vendor, but did not invest the resources to purchase the bogus part.

As agreed with your offices, unless you publicly announce the contents of this report earlier, we plan no further distribution until 30 days from the report date. At that time, we will send copies to the appropriate congressional committees, the Acting Under Secretary of Defense for Acquisition, Technology, and Logistics, and other interested parties. In addition, the report will be available at no charge on the GAO website at http://www.gao.gov.

If you or your staff have any questions about this report or need additional information, please contact Richard Hillman at (202) 512-6722 or hillmanr@gao.gov or Timothy Persons at (202) 512-6522 or personst@gao.gov. Contact points for our Offices of Congressional Relations and Public Affairs may be found on the last page of this report. Other key contributors to this report are listed in appendix II.

Richard J. Hillman
Managing Director
Forensic Audits and Investigative Service

Timothy Persons
Chief Scientist
U.S. Government Accountability Office

Appendix I: Details of Authentication Analysis Tests

This appendix provides details on each of the tests that constitute the authentication analysis SMT Corp. conducted for the parts we purchased.

Visual inspection: Visual inspection is performed on a predetermined number of samples (usually 100 percent) to look for legitimate nonconformance issues as well as any red flags commonly found within suspect counterfeit devices.

Resistance to solvents (RTS): A mixture of mineral spirits and isopropyl alcohol is used to determine the part marking resistance and pure acetone is used to remove any resurface material. This test is not performed on all parts. In some cases, resurfacing material would not be used by counterfeiters to re-mark a part; in others, the solvents would remove markings even on legitimate parts.

X-ray florescence (XRF) elemental analysis: The XRF gathers and measures the elements within a target area. This is used specifically for testing components for RoHS or Hi-Rel conformance, which refer to dangerous substances such as lead (Pb), cadmium (Cd), and mercury (Hg) that are commonly used in electronics manufacturing. For suspect counterfeit devices, it helps determine if a component has the correct plating for the specification it supposed to adhere to.

Package configuration and dimensions: This test measures key areas of the device to see if they fall within industry specifications.

Real-time X-ray analysis: X-ray analysis is performed on a predetermined number of samples (usually 100 percent). The internal construction of components is inspected (depending on the component package type) for legitimate issues such as broken/taut bond wires, electrostatic discharge damage, broken die, and so forth. For suspect counterfeit devices, the differences in die size/shape, lead frames, bond wire layout, and so forth are inspected.

Scanning electron microscopy: A scanning electron microscope is used to perform an exterior visual inspection—more in depth than the previous visual inspection. This is usually performed on a two-piece sample from the evidence lot. Depending on the package type, indications of suspect counterfeit devices are sought, including surface lapping, sandblasting, and sanding with regard to part marking removal.

Solderability: This test is usually for legitimate components to determine if they will solder properly when they are used in production.

Dynasolve: Dynasolve is a chemical used to break down epoxies in an effort to remove resurfacing material that is impervious to the standard RTS test.

Decapsulation/delidding and die verification: The die of a component is exposed with either corrosive materials or a cutting apparatus. This is done to inspect the die or "brain" of a component to determine its legitimacy. This process is performed on numerous samples to look for differences between samples, such as die metallization layout, revisions, part numbers, and so forth—all of which are red flags for suspect counterfeit parts.

Appendix II: GAO Contacts and Staff Acknowledgments

GAO Contacts	Richard J. Hillman, (202) 512-6722 or hillmanr@gao.gov Timothy Persons, (202) 512-6522 or personst@gao.gov
Staff Acknowledgments	Cindy Brown Barnes, Assistant Director; Gary Bianchi, Assistant Director; Virginia Chanley; Dennis Fauber; Barbara Lewis; Jeffery McDermott; Maria McMullen; Kimberly Perteet, Analyst in Charge; Ramon Rodriguez; and Timothy Walker made key contributions to this report.

GAO's Mission	The Government Accountability Office, the audit, evaluation, and investigative arm of Congress, exists to support Congress in meeting its constitutional responsibilities and to help improve the performance and accountability of the federal government for the American people. GAO examines the use of public funds; evaluates federal programs and policies; and provides analyses, recommendations, and other assistance to help Congress make informed oversight, policy, and funding decisions. GAO's commitment to good government is reflected in its core values of accountability, integrity, and reliability.
Obtaining Copies of GAO Reports and Testimony	The fastest and easiest way to obtain copies of GAO documents at no cost is through GAO's website (www.gao.gov). Each weekday afternoon, GAO posts on its website newly released reports, testimony, and correspondence. To have GAO e-mail you a list of newly posted products, go to www.gao.gov and select "E-mail Updates."
Order by Phone	The price of each GAO publication reflects GAO's actual cost of production and distribution and depends on the number of pages in the publication and whether the publication is printed in color or black and white. Pricing and ordering information is posted on GAO's website, http://www.gao.gov/ordering.htm. Place orders by calling (202) 512-6000, toll free (866) 801-7077, or TDD (202) 512-2537. Orders may be paid for using American Express, Discover Card, MasterCard, Visa, check, or money order. Call for additional information.
Connect with GAO	Connect with GAO on Facebook, Flickr, Twitter, and YouTube. Subscribe to our RSS Feeds or E-mail Updates. Listen to our Podcasts. Visit GAO on the web at www.gao.gov.
To Report Fraud, Waste, and Abuse in Federal Programs	Contact: Website: www.gao.gov/fraudnet/fraudnet.htm E-mail: fraudnet@gao.gov Automated answering system: (800) 424-5454 or (202) 512-7470
Congressional Relations	Katherine Siggerud, Managing Director, siggerudk@gao.gov, (202) 512-4400, U.S. Government Accountability Office, 441 G Street NW, Room 7125, Washington, DC 20548
Public Affairs	Chuck Young, Managing Director, youngc1@gao.gov, (202) 512-4800 U.S. Government Accountability Office, 441 G Street NW, Room 7149 Washington, DC 20548